Relationships

Dr. Mark R. Naim

BALBOA
PRESS
A DIVISION OF HAY HOUSE

Balboa Press books may be ordered through booksellers or by contacting:

Balboa Press
A Division of Hay House
1663 Liberty Drive
Bloomington, IN 47403
www.balboapress.com.au
1-(877) 407-4847

ISBN: 978-1-4525-0662-3 (sc)
ISBN: 978-1-4525-0665-4 (e)

Printed in the United States of America

Balboa Press rev. date: 08/13/2012

For Roberta

who showed me what love is

Contents

Acknowledgements

I would especially like to thank Dr Jennifer Hunter for her constant support, and incisive comments regarding what this book is really all about. I also wish to thank Rebecca Baldwin and Jack Lagan for their willingness to proof read the manuscript and help raise it to a standard that I couldn't.

I want to thank and acknowledge my teachers, especially Brandon Bays; Kevin Billet; Caroline Myss; Rabbi Noson Weiss (Jerusalem); Rabbi Simon Jacobson (New York); and Robert Kremnizer—who started me off on this journey.

I want to thank my sister Linda Goldsheft, a world-class cake creator and graphic designer, who has never failed to provide loving support and good artistic advice.

And then there are all of those other people who don't know how much they have touched and instructed me. But I know who you are, and you have my daily thanks.

Introduction

Relationships are a fundamental part of life. They are part of what motivates us, part of what helps move and direct us to be who we are and do the things we do. They help bring meaning and purpose into our lives. They can be mystical, and a source of joy; they can allow one to be known intimately and accepted by another—weaknesses and all, and can allow one to experience a deep sense of being "home".

It is part of the function of any meaningful relationship to provide the potential, opportunity and environment to help us learn and grow as human beings, to help us change as we need to with time, and be the best people we can be.

It is by using the experiences that arise within the context of partnership—both joyful and painful ones—that we come to embrace the enormous spiritual capacity that lies within us, making us capable of magnificent things, not only in the area of relationships, but in every area of life.
—Kathy Freston

We all love being heard. When we are able to feel accepted—either singly, or in a group—we tend to be happy. We all love being loved.

When people love you, they will want to help you—in your personal life and in your business. Your chances of succeeding in life are much greater.

But, when we shut down, when we give up or compromise ourselves, when we deny or suppress what we really think, feel or want—and behave in a way or say things that we don't necessarily mean—problems arise. We do this to get or keep the company of others, or when we think we are not worthy. If we do shut down, or give up, we can end up feeling very sad and sorry for ourselves as a result.

The dysfunctional relationships we form in this state of being will inevitably press all our hot buttons, and be a source of frustration, anger, loneliness and misery.

We can end up feeling alone—something we all hate. We can be in a room full of people, including family or friends, or be walking down a crowded street, and yet still feel a sense of aloneness and disconnection.

When relationships are not working, people can feel confused and lost. They have a need to find some kind of help that will cut through the mess and shine a light on what to think, what to feel, where to go, and what to do.

The challenge, therefore, has always been to find out why we sometimes end up in this state of confusion, feeling alone. We always need to understand why we are not in the meaningful relationship we want to be in, or why the present one we have is not working.

In order to find answers to these questions, including the reasons for problems arising in the first place, I began to ask questions such as the following:

> Why do we have relationships?
> Why are they necessary or needed?
> What do they bring into our lives?
> How can we understand them?
> What are their strengths and weaknesses?
> And especially, what should we do when relationships we are in get into trouble or break down?

It seems that now—in this 'energy age' of rapid change, the Internet and instant communication—we are experiencing accelerating change. Everything is moving faster; everything seems to be intensified. What took past generations a lifetime to understand and achieve, we may now learn in ten to twenty years.

Because of these rapidly changing times, many of us will have more than one major relationship in this lifetime. By that I mean a primary committed relationship, such as marriage.

When we live with our extended family or tribe, we would normally have many important and supportive relationships. Nowadays, however, many of us live in so-called satellite units, removed from our family. If this is the case, the prime relationships we do have take on extra meaning and are more critical for our well-being.

In view of all this, what I have attempted to do is the following:

1. Examine the factors that come into play in our lives, find out how those factors influence the choices we make and the relationships we have.

2. Create a framework on which the subject of relationships could be examined, and then make this information available and shared as simply and as practically as possible.

3. Use this information that we have at our disposal and decide what actions to take, whether we need to find, maintain or repair a relationship.

This book is not meant to be a quick fix, full of ready answers or solutions for relationship problems.

The aim is to be able to help people understand why problems exist in their relationships—either with others or themselves—to find answers that work for them, and to help them make changes for the better.

The real goal then is to be able to create those relationships we want, which should be healthy, meaningful, joyful and fulfilling.

> *Great relationships make great people*
> *—AC Grayling*

Thus, this book . . .

Reasons for Relationships

This chapter (and all the others) is based on all my study, from evidence that is available from multiple sources, plus of course my own experience. The ideas that follow are what I have come to believe is true.

Basically, the substance of the universe—the glue that holds it all together—is love. Before we are born into this physical world, we are all intimately part of this love, this creative energy. Without the flow of this loving energy, we (and the entire universe) would cease to exist.

For us to exist in physicality and come into being as people, it is required that we seemingly separate from this love. I say *seemingly*, because we never really do. It is an illusion that we need, in order to exist as individuals, with free will.

However, before we choose to separate and be conceived and born, we have the ability to choose what we need to experience in the life to come—for our continued growth as beings, and for the perfection of the physical world.

To help with this, we set up agreements with ourselves, and other souls. These agreements (or contracts) form the basis of the major relationships we will have in the life to come and the circumstances that arise from them. I think that if we understand this, everything that happens subsequently has meaning and makes sense.

We are also given certain skills to help us. This includes our intelligence, personality type and natural abilities. It also includes our intuition or ability to energetically assess other people, and the ability to receive all the help that is made available for us.

In addition, before birth, we are specifically required to forget everything. Part of what has to happen is that we come into this world without any recollection of where we come from or which agreements have been made. This is so we can use the attribute of choice.

Choice

We must be free to exercise choice in this world and to experience the consequences of our choices—including those that come from relationships.

If we were born knowing what was going to happen to us, life would not hold any challenges. We would forfeit the chance to grow through overcoming these challenges, and that would make existence meaningless.

Having choice is not the same as being in control. Control is usually fear-based. By trying to control everything in our world, we actually impose a cage or set of restrictions on ourselves, and this limits our experiences, and therefore our development and growth as human beings. What we need to know is that control is actually beyond control.

We can choose to stay in openness instead, and embrace the unknown at all times. In this way we open ourselves to the abundance that life offers, and the unlimited possibilities that exist.

The most foolish thing in Life is to give up choice.
Choice and Power—they are the only two things in life.
Not Love. Love is the quality of the manner in which
you conduct yourself.
—Deepak Chopra

We will come to know who we are through what we choose in this life.

Discovering Yourself

Perhaps the most important reason for having relationships is to discover (or re-discover) who we are. The goal is to live fully and vibrantly as human beings as an expression of who we are in this physical world. I have described other ways of finding out who you are later in the book, in chapter 17.

But for now, in light of the above, when considering relationships a key requirement is to ask the following:

1. Who am I?
2. Where am I going?
3. Who is going with me?

And the important thing is—not to change the order.

The answers to these questions can guide you, and place you in a much healthier position to choose an appropriate partner or fellow traveller for yourself. They may share the same vision or goal, but if (more likely) they don't, they will have qualities that will help you to learn and be who you are, and assist you to go where you need to go. The rest follows and can be worked out.

In an ideal world, this would be the way to go. And yet, even if someone who is apparently not the right one enters your life, he or she will still help you learn who you are—if you are open to that.

It may be more of a rocky road than a smooth one, but it is still your road, and the result (of helping you to become more of who you are) can be the same.

There is also another, more reflective approach. Rather than asking: "Who shall I choose to come with me?" you could ask the question, "Who has been chosen for me, and why?"

This approach can leave you open to guidance, and the question enables you to step back and choose more wisely and objectively than you may have done otherwise.

In life, and in relationships, it's important to keep things going well by going where you are meant to go. If you're not going where you are meant to go before a relationship begins, then you may not ever find out where you are meant to go afterwards—and the relationship will almost certainly go nowhere.

What this little play on words means is that we had better not give up on who we are in order to make a relationship work. If we do that we will lose who we are, and the relationship will not work anyway. You cannot abandon yourself in order to find yourself.

"To thine own self be true" becomes a working framework that can't be ignored. It is necessary to have the ability to be your own observer and be aware of how and why you do the things you do, think the way you think, and feel the way you feel.

Be who you are and say what you feel because those who mind don't matter and those who matter don't mind.
—Bernard M Baruch

Once you are clear about the above, then it becomes easier to ask what the real purpose of having relationships with others, is.

Relationships work best when you always do what is best for you—this realisation is a life-altering insight.

Key Relationships

We need to look more closely at why we have a few very special relationships in our lives. What is the point? How come they are special, and so important? Why do we want these relationships so much? Why have them at all?

Do we have them to help us heal our wounds, or to help heal someone else's? Do they exist to provide meaning and purpose in our lives? Do we need a witness to validate our feelings or thoughts (or even allow them)? Do we have relationships to fill a sense of aloneness or emptiness, or to give us a sense of where we belong? Do we just need to feel safe with another? Do they exist to give us a steady platform and feeling of security from which we can go out into life?

Do we need another to experience the giving and receiving of love, to remind us of where we come from, and to feel alive? Do we need another to reflect back to us who we are being at any one time?

Do we have to be with someone else to feel special, or feel connected with humanity?

Relationships can be about any or all of these things, of course. Remember that as souls, we all come from a place of oneness, where we are all interconnected. Therefore it's not that we can choose whether we want to have relationships; they are inevitable. What we can choose is the particular type of relationship that suits us at any one time, one that helps us to become more of who we are, and less of who we are not.

The following is an often-quoted and beautiful short essay, by an anonymous author:

People come into our lives for a reason, a season, or a lifetime.
When someone is in your life for a REASON, it is usually to meet a need you have expressed. They have come to assist you through a difficulty, to provide you with guidance and support, to aid you physically, emotionally, or spiritually. They may seem like a godsend, and they are. They are there for the reason you need them to be. Then, without any wrongdoing on your part, or at an inconvenient time, this person will say or do something to bring the relationship to an end. Sometimes they die. Sometimes they walk away. Sometimes they act up and force you to take a stand. One way or another, when that need has been met, it becomes time for you to move on.

Some people come into your life for a SEASON, because your turn has come to share, grow or learn. They bring you an experience of peace or make you laugh. They may teach you something you have never done. They usually give you an unbelievable amount of joy. Believe it, it is real.

But only for a season.

LIFETIME relationships teach you lifetime lessons, things you must build upon in order to have a solid emotional foundation. Your job is to accept the lesson, love the person and put what you have learned to use in all other relationships and areas of your life. It is said that love is blind but friendship is clairvoyant.

I would say in addition:

The purpose of any healthy relationship is to provide a safe space in which to experience who you really are. Experiencing who you are is why you are here; it is the purpose of all life.

Your sacred space is where you can find yourself again and again.
—Joseph Campbell

Finding yourself is achieved through what you put into a relationship, not what you want out of it. It is in the giving of who you are that you will benefit from the best experience a relationship has to offer.

Remember this: you can't change someone to suit your apparent needs in a relationship. They will always revert to their natural character sooner or later. If a relationship was created on that basis, it is not likely to survive, at least not meaningfully.

It is in the safe space of a relationship that we can look at our discomforts and our fears, and work on them. The energy that guides and looks after this, is love. In general, it is much easier (or more acceptable) to hear something about ourselves that needs attention, from someone who cares for us and has our well-being at heart.

In addition, we often attract into our lives those who mirror the energy we are putting out at the time. So if we are feeling insecure about ourselves, we may attract into our lives someone who feels the same way. Their presence will force us to address that particular issue.

Troubled relationships can therefore be the sign that something within us needs attention. If we don't learn a lesson the first time around, the person involved will probably move on. We are then likely to attract (or be attracted to) exactly the same kind of person the next time, until we learn what we need to learn. Once learned, we are free to move on.

In the space of any relationship, as you receive feedback about yourself, the ideal behaviour is to stay in that space and not ignore what you are being told. Welcome the thoughts and feelings that arise in response, and then explore options to deal with them. This is not always easy; we will inevitably have our "hot buttons" pressed, and we may want to "shoot the messenger"!

It is useful to remember however, that you (as an individual) have all the tools and resources you need to deal with every challenge that will arise in life. It is a matter of understanding, trust and faith, until experience confirms it.

This then is the canvas on which we paint our lives, with all the relationships that will be part of it.

Whatever relationships we have, with whatever opportunities or challenges they bring, once they have achieved what they were meant to and we complete a contract, that part of us is in balance or healed, and we move on.

I don't believe people are looking for the meaning of life as much as they are looking for the experience of being alive.
—Joseph Campbell

Influences and Attitude

Before we look at what specific influences come into our lives, it is worth making some general comments.

There will be influences that come into our lives to which we are obliged to respond. These influences can be opportunities that excite us and are close to our passions, or they can be stumbling blocks that cause us to experience various difficulties. Relationships are one of the ways in which these influences are provided.

To recognise what these influences are, to be able to work with them and see what needs attention and what doesn't, we need to develop the ability to be our own observer. We have to learn to be able to "step outside" an issue and distance ourselves from what is happening, and ask ourselves constantly what the reasons are for what we are experiencing.

"How come this is happening to me? What am I being asked to learn?"

When we can look objectively at what is happening around us and to us (and continuously make corrections to our thinking and behaviour), this allows us to (metaphorically) be in the driver's seat of our life, and not in the passenger's seat.

To do that, we need to be able to recognise and meet our own resistance, and take action. Resistance is, in fact, a subconscious avoidance strategy—most likely to avoid facing what we fear. Taking appropriate action can be difficult to do effectively all the time, but doing this is the path to achieving the most amazing and rewarding results in your life.

Remember the laws of the universe:

"That which you resist, persists. That which you fight you make stronger. That which you look at, disappears. What you focus on, grows; whatever you judge, you will become.
—Anonymous

When we stay with our feelings or thoughts and play with them, try to suppress them, or collapse into them, we give them a life that demands time and energy from us. This distracts us from our real purpose and function. It is like trying to keep a balloon under water. It takes constant attention and energy; as soon as we become distracted, the balloon pops up, and we have to go through the whole process of pushing it down again. This can be exhausting.

We always have free choice—to follow our thoughts, collapse and become them, or to stay still and let them come and go. We are not our thoughts; we are not our feelings—we are who we are.
—Brandon Bays, founder of The Journey Organization
(Reference 1)

If we understand that we are not our thoughts, nor our feelings, and we merely let them come and go, then we remain connected to our true selves, our essence. This enables us to be grounded, strong and centred in the moment.

Truth loves you so much that in each moment it gives you the opportunity to choose whether you follow your thoughts or stay still and let them pass through.
—Brandon Bays

It is, therefore, always better to welcome whatever uncomfortable experiences and feelings come your way, surrender to them and fully experience them. In this way you can come to understand that they have no power over you unless you give them that power. This leaves you free to be yourself.

Struggling through life's terrors is the key to true liberation; these terrors are life's great teachers. Liberation is not an end in itself, but a pathway to the deepest essence of self.
—Gaby Burt, The Journey

In the Womb

If this is the general plan, how does it all unfold in reality?

After conception, the first relationship we have is the one with our mother, during the period of gestation in the womb. This world is rich with energy of all kinds.

The emotional environment that the developing baby experiences whilst in the womb matters very much. There is no doubt that the mother's emotional state whilst pregnant has a profound effect on the baby—as well as all the usual factors, including biochemical, physiological, and genetic.

It is possible to take a person back, using guided imagery or similar techniques, to the time before they were born. In this state, the person can experience the emotional state that was their reality in the womb.

You can do this yourself. Sit in a quiet place, close your eyes, take your awareness into your body, and pick a strong feeling that you find there. It may or may not be a feeling you are very familiar with; it doesn't really matter. Starting with that, gently take your awareness back down through the years, noting whether or not this feeling was present at each age. Sometimes one isn't sure—again that doesn't matter. Just keep going. Some feeling will always be present.

Count the years literally. Once you have counted down to birth (keeping your awareness on how you were feeling at the time) go back into the womb. Staying aware, there will be one overriding feeling. For example, if your mother generally felt contentment and harboured love for the unborn child within, you will feel that. A state of peace, love, acceptance and warmth prevails.

On the other hand, if your mother was in a state of anxiety or fear for example, then you may sense anxiety in yourself. This anxiety might stem from her tendency to worry all the time, or from some traumatic event during the pregnancy. I have worked with people in this way who describe themselves as being chronically anxious, and have been so from birth.

When helping people take their awareness back to their intra-uterine experience, several recalled vividly that their mother was very unhappy during the pregnancy because of some kind of abuse. Other people have recalled an unhappy intra-uterine experience because they were unwanted, and subsequently given away for adoption after birth.

In several other examples, people have described being anxious all their lives. Their intra-uterine experience was one of anxiety. Their mother was an anxious person, and *her* mother had been the same, and so on. This form of anxiety is a generational phenomenon, with each person unaware of where it comes from; it is just there.

If you reflect on this for a moment, you can see how profound this emotional environment is. You can see how this experience (and subsequent embedded feelings) could govern and influence the entire life of a person.

There are also sensations and impressions gained from being born. For the great majority of people, this isn't an issue. There is, however, the very occasional individual who is literally filled with fear just before, during, or just after the birth process. That again, can have life-enduring consequences.

People have been able to recall memories of trauma around birth, including asphyxiation, falling, being dropped, or being born in a strange place where the mother was in great distress. In all cases, the baby experienced a sense of fear and panic. This feeling remained as body memory (*Robin Grille, reference 2)* until the person sought help as an adult, to clear issues that had arisen as a consequence of these early influences.

Our experiences in life start here, and this influence is as strong as anything else we encounter along the way. A healthy, loving mother-child relationship is where we first learn what love and closeness is, and its protective value stays with us all our lives.

Experiences we have in this period (plus the first few years afterwards) also have a strong influence on the type of attachment style we have with other people in the future.

The Early Years

Using what we know of child development, I have focussed here on what can happen when things go wrong—rather than when things go right. Erik Erikson (*Arlene Harder, reference 3*) gives a very clear synopsis of what the developmental stages are in a person, what is normally required, and what the desired outcomes are.

Maria Montessori identified the age that cognitive memory starts in a child. The developing brain has the capacity to absorb certain material quickly, but it seems that we are only able to recall events cognitively from around two to two-and-a-half years of age. (There are however, a few individuals who have clear memories from an even earlier age.) Before this time though, experiences are largely emotionally based, and are stored as such in the body. Therapies dealing with these very early memories would therefore (by definition) have to be emotionally based.

Children tend to be very quick at coming to some sort of conclusion about themselves and others around them, based on their experiences. And the age of the child is no barrier to the formation of beliefs about his or her world and him—or herself.

There are countless stories about memories that have been elicited from adults (under therapy conditions) from their very early years, that they otherwise were not able to recall. Some of these are dealt with in the next chapter.

As we get older, we develop the ability to store complex information in our brains, which can be recalled later in life. If the memories we have about an experience are pleasant, we tend to be able to recall many or all of its details.

However, if something happens to us that is unpleasant, we may not want to remember it. We may even go into a degree of shutdown, so there is no (or very little) cognitive or mind component to the memory.

Or we may have a recollection of the event, but find that the reactions and feelings associated with that event have been blocked out, and can't be remembered when we try to think about it.

Our ability to store that information in our bodies is not compromised however, and this energy is somehow kept in a form that is congruent with the original experience.

Under the right conditions then, this information is (still) available to us, and can be used to see what influence it has had on us in terms of beliefs, behaviour or attitudes in later life. We can then decide whether they are healthy or not, and whether we need to keep them.

This theme is explored more in the next chapter, concentrating on those things that have stopped us from being who we really are and having the relationships we want.

Beliefs and Vows

When we have an experience (apart from the memory of the event) we often form an opinion about what happened, or form a belief or make promises or vows to ourselves as a result of that event, especially if it was unpleasant.

Beliefs govern our thinking, and underlie much of our emotions and behaviour. If we want to change our behaviour, or the way we react—either to events or people—we may need to find out what our core beliefs are. The beliefs relating to that behaviour may have very likely come from experiences we have had earlier in our lives.

Belief systems can originate from various sources, and we may even have beliefs that conflict with one another. They can interfere with our well-being and cause all sorts of stresses.

Becoming entrenched in beliefs that no longer serve us can keep us in a state of duality and put us in a constant state of judgment.
—Anita Moorjani

I have come across countless stories of belief systems that were set up, often as children, that ran contrary to the nature and well-being of the person concerned. They may have adopted a belief as a direct result of a traumatic experience, or they may have been convinced in other ways that this is the way life really functions.

We all recognise these beliefs and they often turn out like this: "I'm not good enough"; "I'm not loveable"; "I have to be quiet"; "I can't trust anyone"; and so on.

We may come to believe that it is possible to miss out on our needs. Here's a classic: "If you are good, you will get". Almost all of us subscribe to this one to some extent. There is a fear of missing out on our needs if we don't gain the approval of others; we need to prove that we are a worthwhile investment for them in some way.

It's useful therefore to ask yourself what motivates and drives you. And then ask: do those influences affect the way you interact with people, and whether you are happy with the outcomes? For example, does fear propel you into making decisions that go against your inner wisdom, instinct or nature?

Almost certainly, one of the functions of our prime relationship(s) will be to bring these beliefs to the fore, so they can be acknowledged and dealt with. The behaviour resulting from these beliefs inevitably gets in the way of a deeper, more fulfilled relationship. People who care won't let us hide behind this behaviour—they will point it out for us, even if we don't like it.

Here are examples of low-energy personal beliefs that have arisen from general life situations, some of which you may recognize in yourself or others:

> "I'm just no good at that sort of thing"
> "Everyone else seems to have things under control, except me"
> "I regret so many things"
> "I just don't have the confidence that others seem to have"
> "I can never make up my mind"
> "I have to stay strong"
> "My future won't go the way I want it"
> "I will never reach my full potential"
> "Other people always put me down"

Then there are those beliefs that often arise from family pressures and (especially) expectations:

"I have to look after everyone else before
I can look after myself."
"No one pays any attention to me."
"If I fail I will be punished, so I may as
well not even try."
"No one respects me."
"I can never do what I really want to do."
"I'm afraid of failing, or letting someone
down."
"I always make mistakes."
"I'm useless."

Other examples of low-energy beliefs are as follows:

"I always miss out."
"I do not fit in anywhere."
"I can never get things done."
"I can't cope."
"My future will be a disaster."
"I'm fat or ugly or stupid."
"It's too hard to change."
"I have to say or do what the others
want to make them happy."

And add to this list the most telling belief, "I will miss
out if I don't conform."

Physical abuse of one kind or another in life is unfortunately very common, especially involving women and children. This abuse can lead to the formation of beliefs such as:

> "There is something wrong with me."
> "I will never speak out again."
> "That abuse has ruined my life."
> "No one believes me."
> "I can't be honest with people."
> "I will hide and no one will ever find me again."
> "I will never be able to trust again."
> "If I fight back, I will be killed or harmed; I must be submissive."
> "No one will ever really want me."
> "Being touched is disgusting."

What follows are several examples of belief systems (generalised from a very large number of stories) that were formed at various ages. I have described briefly how these beliefs manifested later on in life and how they severely affected the lives and relationships of the people involved.

1. A woman presented with an infertility problem, which badly affected her marital relationship. She was able to access a memory of herself in her early

teens, in which she was abused, and when she tried to tell her story no one believed her.

She formed a belief as a result of that experience that life wasn't fair, and decided that she would never allow this to happen to her children. In her mind, she wanted children; at a subconscious level, she shut down her reproductive system.

2. A middle-aged man presented who was very shy, with an inability to get close to anyone. He was able to recall an event in his life as a child when he got into trouble for speaking his mind. As a result of this event he promised himself he would never speak up again, for fear of making a mistake. He couldn't be open with people for the same reason. He distanced himself from people so as not to risk being hurt.

3. One woman presented in her fifties in a deep depression. She had been raped as a child, and she had not been believed when she tried to tell her mother. As a result of this experience, she made a promise to herself: "I must be quiet and stay in the background so no one will ever find me again". Her rage was never expressed—containing this within herself became a large part of the cause of her depression. The relationship with her mother

disintegrated early on. In addition, because she had a poor sense of personal boundaries, she fell into several abusive relationships as an adult. This is an all-too-common story.

4. Another woman in her fifties presented with relationship difficulties, including the fact that she didn't like being touched. She had ambivalent feelings towards her husband, and the marriage eventually fell apart. It came out in her story that as a child, she had never been held or told that she was loved by either parent. She just didn't know how to express love, or receive it. She believed she was not worthy of being loved, and of course under these circumstances, her marriage could not sustain itself.

She had another belief as well (because her father had been unfaithful): "You can't trust a man." This had an equally negative influence on all her male relationships.

5. A middle-aged man presented with anger, frustration, a sense of meaningless in life, and very low self-esteem. He came from an emotionally dead home where he wasn't valued, and that influenced his relationships all his life—both personally and professionally.

He came to believe as a boy that it doesn't matter how you felt, or what you wanted, no one would notice. He was left with an empty feeling that no matter what he did, he hadn't achieved anything at all in his life.

6. Yet another woman presented with frustration and loneliness, especially in relationships. She had been forced to have oral sex with boys as a child. Her self-talk at the time was: "I had my innocence taken away from me. Why can't I deal with this situation better? I can't trust people."

    She developed a sense of the importance of secrecy, and felt all her life that she had to be submissive and never express her true feelings. She had many male partners over the years, but the relationships never lasted long. She got tired of these men and moved on. It was her way of getting her own back.

7. A middle-aged woman (who was a second child) presented with deep depression that started after the birth of her second child. In therapy, she remembered being alone at home at the age of four, when her mother came back from hospital with a third child. Her self-talk was: "What's going to happen to me? Will there be any time for me? No one is paying any attention to me. I feel like

nothing, and no one will notice me anyway. I will just give up and be by myself".

These feelings of hopelessness and helplessness were all triggered by the birth of her second child.

The important thing here was that she—like most of us—was unaware of the significance of her past experiences until it was revealed much later on.

8. Another woman in her forties had real issues with intimacy and she didn't like physical contact. She was able to recall being 'touched' by her teenage cousin when she was twelve. This interpersonal violence caused her to form a belief that being touched was disgusting!

9. This is another very common story. A man presented, very upset at having been asked for a divorce after an eight-year marriage. He had a background of generally distant family relationships, and a very anxious mother.

It was revealed in therapy that, because of this background, he had set up a 'Cinderella' fantasy as a young man. The fantasy revolved around love, marriage, and living happily ever after, to escape the emotional desert that he came from.

He carried other beliefs of unworthiness, that he was always a failure, and that he was insignificant.

By his thirties, his dream had not materialised. When his wife-to-be came along—even though his intuition told him she wasn't the right one—he was so afraid of not getting his fantasy that he married her nonetheless.

His grief did not derive from the break-up of his relationship so much, as the loss of his fantasy. This belief had to be exposed—and the feelings he had around that, experienced—to allow who he really was and what he really wanted, to be revealed and dealt with.

10. A man (in therapy) recalled a memory of being in his cot as an infant, crying, with soiled, cold clothing. He wanted to be cleaned, picked up and hugged. For some reason, his mother didn't hear him straight away. The baby formed the view in that moment that he was not loved, and he felt abandoned

By the time his mother appeared, this belief was embedded; later in life, abandonment was a big issue, and he had difficulties with trust and relationships.

11. A couple presented, feeling that their relationship was not going anywhere, as if it was 'empty'. One partner would always say something he thought would make the other happy. He would never state his own feelings or preferences. Conversely, his partner would never say anything meaningful, for fear of offending the other. Both people had adopted this behaviour as a result of being humiliated as children and coming to believe that they weren't important. It was if the relationship was invisible, mirroring how each felt about themselves. They felt comfortable with each other in the beginning, as each permitted the attitude of the other.

A very common form of behaviour that we see is the one that comes from a place of perceived emptiness or lack inside. It often comes from unrealistically high expectations imposed on someone—for example from themselves, from family, from peers or from their culture.

Here is such an example. One particular woman held enormous expectations for herself because of her mother's expectations of her. The mother wanted her daughter to achieve all the things she hadn't, to be all the things she had wanted to be and never was.

This woman was "perfect": a talented musician, a prizewinner at school, highly successful professionally, and married to an approved "trophy" husband. She had never followed what her real passions in life were, and eventually found herself unable to maintain the effort of keeping her artificial life going. At the age of forty, it all fell apart, ending with the break-up of her marriage and loss of her job. She started taking drugs to escape her pain, and that's when I met her—jobless, single, penniless, unhappy and depressed.

In this and other similar situations, the person involved tries to live up to these expectations, for fear of not getting the love or approval they want, or to prevent judgement or criticism. These people can present as failures having been unable to live up to expectations. They can also present as extremely successful people materially. The pressures of expectations on these individuals lead to what I call the *have, do, be* syndrome: "I have to *have*, I will *do* what it takes to *have*, and then I will *be* somebody".

Of course, the opposite (*be, do, have*) is the healthier way to live: "I will *be* who I am, I will *do* what it takes to be who I am, and the *have* will automatically take care of itself".

People so affected can drive themselves relentlessly, often with devastating consequences in their emotional and family life. They are often the people who turn around in their forties, and wonder what happened— where their family and life have disappeared to, with no idea why.

There are countless stories of people who have been affected by these kinds of beliefs. When things happen to us that we don't understand or that prove to be hurtful, we react to them—with negative self-talk, beliefs, and vows.

These beliefs and vows then become the underlying programs that run our lives. They can manifest later on with emotional, physical, and psychological distress, or a sense of disconnection to life, and they can powerfully influence relationships.

Once we have learned to let go of all vows and all beliefs, we discover that, in reality, we are part of the unconditional love we have spoken about. We learn that—in fact—we are an individual manifestation of this love. That is the real gift waiting for us. It's just a process of getting there.

Letting Go of Beliefs

We need to consider whether we own our beliefs, or do they own us? Are our beliefs changeable, or not? Are your beliefs so embedded, they can never be shifted? Do you believe today what you believed last year, or even yesterday? Do you believe your beliefs, in fact? Does having any particular belief cause you to be critical or judgemental—against another, or yourself? And if so, is this in your best interests?

When we have beliefs that run our lives—contrary to our nature and character—we will inevitably be placed into positions of conflict with someone else, or ourselves.

This can lead to various states of emotional, psychological and physiological confusion as stated. As a result, we get distracted, energy-depleted and fatigued, run down, and even become prone to illness. We can also become stuck in those states of unwellness.

Correcting this is a journey, taking one step at a time. It starts with an awareness and admission that these beliefs and promises exist, and the knowledge that healing (getting back to your true nature) requires "an absence or suspension of belief and even a letting go of the need to be healed" (*Anita Moorjani, reference 4*). This leads to a state of being open to all possibilities. Then, the infinite resources of the universe—and all the help you need—becomes available to you.

In the first place, finding these memories relies on the following principle:

It seems to be a fact that memory recall happens most clearly when a person is in the same emotional state he or she was in when the original event was first experienced. Thus, it becomes important to be able to access that state in the present time. Only then can the memory be revealed as it happened, and for its underlying power to be exposed.

As well as uncovering the memory of an event, it is also possible to elicit any promises or vows made, or beliefs formed, which may have had profound subsequent effects, as explained. Once revealed, these beliefs or promises to oneself can be released, nullified, or replaced with healthy new ones.

Resolving issues doesn't mean going back, finding out who hurt you, blaming them, and making them suffer as a result. It is all about neutralising the issue entirely, and freeing up everyone involved, principally yourself. Memories can remain, but there will be no reaction to them. They no longer retain the power they once had.

The consequences of not doing this work, leaves open the potential to remain stuck in whatever the issue is. This can lead to a failed relationship for example, or any state of ill health. These programs will continue to work in the background, against your own best interests.

Once these old beliefs or personal vows have been exposed and removed, it is possible to help someone move from a place of relative darkness and collapse, into a world of expansion and possibilities. This leads to a state whereby the person is free to begin to experience his or her true self and real potential.

Remember, illness does not come from what has been done to you. It comes from continuing to feel fear, helplessness, hopelessness, resentment, or rage for example . . . and plotting vengeance against those who hurt you. Think about it!

The greatest discovery of any generation is that human beings can alter their lives by altering their attitudes of mind.
—Albert Schweitzer

Nurture to Nature

We have looked at the origin and meaning of relationships, the reasons we chose to be born into this life, what early influences affect the nature of that life, and what the consequences may be.

The next step is to look at the nature of relationships. This includes understanding what the emotional components of an individual are, how they are fundamental in determining the make up of who we are, how we behave—including the development of our relationship style (*Levine and Heller, reference 5*). It also includes an understanding of the mechanics of a relationship.

After that, we can look at issues that exist around relationship problems, and learn what can be done about them.

The Emotional Structure
of People

This approach is based on my understanding of the spiritual energy that exists which goes to form the essence of who we are as human beings (*Simon Jacobson, reference 6*). There are seven basic emotional attributes from which we are all formed. Each person will have one attribute that is their strongest, yet all of us are made up from a combination of all of them. Each attribute has characteristics of all the others as well, each part contributing to and giving its essence to the whole. This results in each of us being the complex unique individuals we are.

These are the true emotions of each human being—unlike those feelings that we commonly call emotions, such as fear, sadness or anger. These feelings are really ego—or personality-based, and not spiritually based.

It is the flow of energy from these attributes that creates the totality of our emotional makeup, with balance in the system as the ideal state. (*Emotion* being *e-motion* or *energy in motion*).

If there is an imbalance, there may be a tendency to overly express yourself in some ways, or not enough in others. This can lead to problems in the way you interrelate with others.

Doing a self-diagnosis by looking at each of the following parts can help identify which areas need attention—to find that harmony and balance—which will enable you to express yourself fully as who you really are in this life.

The following is a simple diagram of how this energy flows from one emotion to the next, each level modifying the ones before with its own special energy, and then contributing to the onward flow.

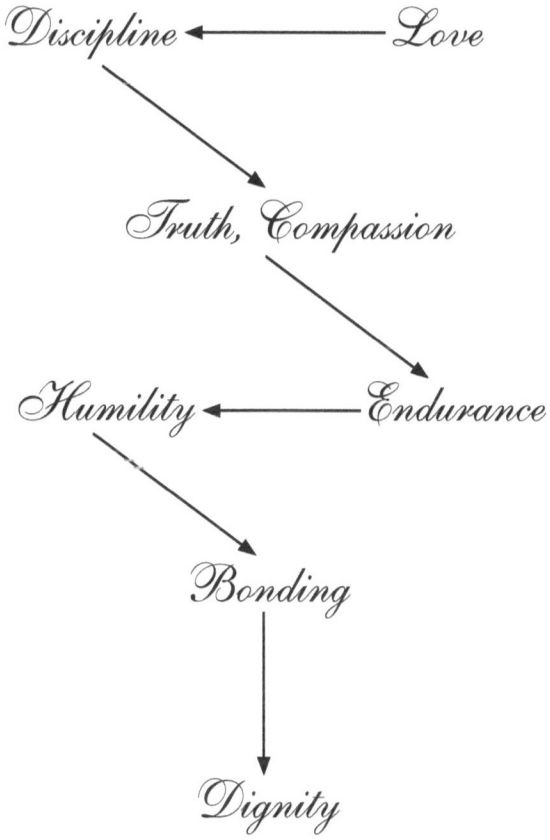

The first six attributes are energy states. The seventh—as an expression of all of them—is where action takes place, where spiritual energy is brought into physicality. It is still a state of *being*, but where the *doing* takes care of itself. Speech resides here as well.

Love

Starting with the basics, all healthy relationships are based on love. This, or aspects of it—such as kindness—is the basis of everything in the universe. It enables us to reach outside ourselves, to cross boundaries; it is the vehicle through which all communication takes place.

A healthy love is expressed for its own sake, because it is there to be expressed. It is not expressed with the intention of expecting anything in return. It is unconditional.

If one experiences (gives and receives) love for the sake of it without qualification, that automatically makes it all and everything (in its purest sense). It's like money: keeping it hidden or unused makes it useless; it has to go around.

Love is neither just nor merciful. It is just what it is: love.

Universal love is beyond limitation; it is undefinable. To think otherwise is to separate yourself from this love. However, in the real world, we have to take account of human frailty and imperfection.

An unhealthy love, for example, can come from a place of emptiness that needs to be filled. It is conditional: "If I give, I must receive—or hope I will receive". Another variant can be this: "I will be the best in my field, and if I am, then you will love me. If I'm not the best, then I am nothing".

Or: "I can elicit love and compassion from you by showing you my pain". This is a so-called secondary gain. Examine your own relationships. Do you love unconditionally, or are there conditions attached?

Love has to be enduring. It has to be able to withstand challenges and setbacks, regardless of the ups and downs of life. It must be trusted to be there and counted on when times are tough. Sometimes it has to be fought for and earned.

Healthy love includes the ability to forgive. It includes the ability to transcend and overlook another's behaviour that may have been unacceptable. It allows us to know that the other person was probably doing the best he or she could, with the resources they had available at the time.

It also recognises the privilege of being able to love and perhaps receive more than you give. Ask yourself if your love has rules, or exists regardless.

Mature love comes with (and brings) personal dignity. It allows you to know your special place in this world. It is neither demoralising nor destructive. It has a sense of freedom that is boundless.

Which is the most effective expression of love? Are all approaches necessary?

Discipline

Do we live in a world of mercy tempered by justice, or do we live in a world of justice tempered by mercy?

It seems that in the greater sense of things, the world is one of absolute truth and justice, which is tempered by mercy. This situation enables humankind to exist, despite its faults and weaknesses.

At the personal level, this tends to swing around. We create relationships based on mercy, tempered by justice. We live in a world where the qualities of love, compassion, and tolerance have been proven to be successful in helping us deal with relationships. Yet these qualities have to be governed by clear, healthy boundaries and appropriate behaviour.

Healthy love always has an element of appropriateness about it inclusive of respect for the other. It also carries an awareness of the other's needs, and capacity to give and receive. It needs discretion.

For example, imagine a parent who, when asked, gives his or her child a sweet. And then another. At some point, the answer has to be no. The child can't see it, but the parent can see potential problems, such as dental care needed down the road.

Which is the act of greater love, saying yes or saying no?

Is your love smothering, or does it include space that allows you to appreciate and respect the other person?

Imagine what your relationships would be like if they were based solely on this quality. Would they be healthy, or ruthless and unforgiving?

Discipline is needed to do what the moment really requires; control is trying to impose your will over what the moment requires.

Harmony, Truth

Truth is the result of love and discipline operating together. Truth is a manifestation of selflessness. It provides a perspective that is beyond the immediate needs of the personality or ego.

It starts to address questions about why we really act in the way we do and say the things we say. We need to understand what our real underlying truths are, to know what we really want, who we really are, and how to express ourselves in the healthiest ways.

Truth is also unchanging. The truth of who you are does not change. If something can change—beliefs for example—then by definition they can't be true. Some beliefs can be relatively 'true', or merely expedient.

This truth also allows compassion for others, and for ourselves. It enables us to find peace within ourselves. A very useful piece of wisdom in this regard is, "Make yourself wrong and the other right".

Are we true to our truths? Do we honour ourselves at all times, or do we compromise ourselves with the inner saboteur (or any of the other archetypes)? Do we sell ourselves short, by trying to please others, or denying ourselves?

This creates an opening and allows us to understand ourselves better. This principle allows us to own and take responsibility for our behaviour, and do something about it. Asking the question, "What must I do to accommodate the other?" or "What am I being asked to learn here?" are also useful attributes to help us along the journey to discover our truths.

These are tough questions that you can ask yourself, but if you can arrive at true answers, you will find a freedom that can't even be imagined.

Endurance

This is the will to persist, to be tenacious, to be steadfast, to overcome. It is a healthy balance of patience, persistence and courage; it is being reliable and accountable. This establishes security and commitment.

It is the readiness to fight for what you believe in, to go all the way. It is the ability to recognise your passions, to be committed to your values, and to follow them no matter what. Life can be at its most electric, be the most exciting, when you choose to step out of your comfort zone and follow your passion—no matter what.

The moment one definitely commits oneself, then Providence moves too. All sorts of things occur to help one that would otherwise never have occurred. A whole stream of events issue from that decision, raising in one's favour all manner of unforseen incidents and meetings and material assistance, which no one would have dreamt would have come their way. Boldness has genius, power and magic in it.
—W.H Murray (Scottish climber of Everest)

Humility

Humility comes from recognising your weaknesses and strengths. It comes from working with your strengths and accepting and minimising your weaknesses.

It comes from understanding that you may not be doing the best you can with the gifts and talents you have, and therefore you should always be striving to do better.

It is not false modesty, putting yourself down, or "playing small". It is recognising and accepting that if someone else had precisely your gifts, perhaps he or she would do a better job than you.

Humility is a blend of all the qualities already mentioned, and also includes the elements of stillness, silence and reverence. Great leaders have this quality.

Bonding

Only now does this quality come into its own importance. Having blended all the above qualities and put them into place, bonding can happen safely. This is the desire and the ability to join with another, to leave separateness and welcome commitment.

This is the acceptance of openness and vulnerability, where one can experience real joy. It is also the acceptance of the possibility of hurt.

This is where the totality of feelings can be experienced. This is where the sense of belonging lives, where togetherness lives. This is where trust develops and grows; this is where self-confidence and self-acceptance come from. In short, this is where we really start to grow as human beings.

This is where we get our first real experience of attachment, where we develop further our attachment style.

Dignity

Dignity is a state of grace, of majesty, and is the consequence of living as an embodiment of the previous six energies. It is where we reach a state of *being*, rather than a state of *doing*. In the state of *being*, the *doing* takes care of itself.

This can be described in the following way: We are human *beings* not human *doings*. In fact, we are not even human beings, but rather human *becomings*.

It is a place where we learn that we matter, that we are unique, that we can make a difference. It is also a state where speech resides. It therefore embodies the ability to create something outside yourself.

Mechanics of a Relationship

Having discussed the energetic makeup of a human being, we can now move on to the practical aspects of the structure of relationships.

How do relationships work, and how do they present the challenges we must inevitably face for our own personal growth? What happens when they work, and what happens when they break down? How do we understand and learn everything we need to from them?

To answer these questions, I find it very useful to have a visual or diagrammatic representation to look at the various elements of a relationship. It is simplistic, but a convenient place to start, to help people understand some of the mechanics, and where they might find themselves at any one time. This can help cut through any confusion that may exist, especially where there are troublesome issues to be solved.

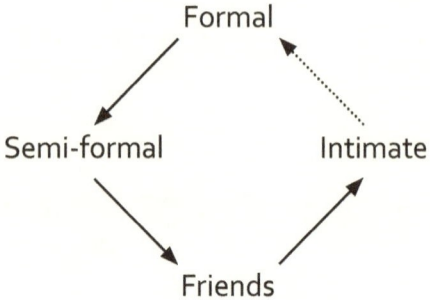

I describe it in this way: relationships usually start formally. There are initial greetings, pleasantries, and enquiries about the basics. It's a kind of grounding exercise. One of the inevitable questions we ask when meeting someone for the first time is, "What do you do?" or "Where do you come from?" It is a safe place to start, and places the person in his or her tribe, culture or community.

As things progress, the relationship moves into a semi-formal stage where one exchanges more personal information. Openness starts here.

The relationship can then move on to a friendship, which involves very personal communication, trust, a high degree of openness and sharing feelings, and of course there is the potential to be vulnerable.

Finally, the relationship can become close, and a commitment to share on all levels can arise. I'm not talking here about lust, or pure physical attraction. I am talking about an intimacy based on an acceptance of the other and a willingness to deepen the relationship.

The speed at which this occurs varies of course, from a slow and steady progression through the stages to love at first sight. In the latter case trust and intimacy can be established very early on, and the learning about the individual comes later. It's not that the progression through the stages is reversed; rather the people involved go around the circle many more times!

As you progress through the stages, it's really worth having a checklist of values that are essential (or unacceptable) to you that you can tick off. This may help avoid scrambling to fix something later on, when it may be much harder.

Later on we will look at relationship repair. It is useful however, to use this simple diagram when looking at any issue that can arise in any relationship. One can go back to *formal*, and look objectively at the issue and ask yourself how important it is to you. Consider how much you are attached to it. Is it a belief you are clinging on to, despite your obvious best interests? What would it be like if you let go, or agree to a compromise?

Once closeness or intimacy has been established—or once a decision has been made to go onwards—people can enter what many authors have described as the five stages of a relationship. These stages vary somewhat from source to source, but include the same essential qualities. The following is an abbreviated version:

Stage one—The romantic stage (or courtship), in which the accent is on sameness and finding similarities. Everything is idealised, beautiful, and happy. Partners are usually blind to any problems here.

Stage two—The stage in which differences and individuality start to surface—where the partner is not seen as perfect. There is a struggle to define respective roles in the relationship. Boundaries start to emerge, and the real work of building the relationship begins. There is a decrease in the intensity of the relationship and an increase in emotional distance. There is a risk of the partner being seen as selfish or uncaring.

Stage three—The stage of challenges and re-evaluation. This is where a sense of disconnection or disillusionment arises; freedom and personal choice become paramount. This is often where one is asked to decide whether the relationship can continue or not.

Stage four—The stage of stability and transformation. Having worked through issues, choices can now be made based on knowledge of self, and the other. Boundaries are generally healthy, and it is a relatively peaceful state.

Stage five—The stage in which each person moves out into the world as a whole person, non-dependant, with mutual warmth, understanding and respect. This is where their paths are individual but parallel, where one supports the other. Needs are met, and the partners stay in the relationship by choice (without outside influences).

It seems that we move through these stages in a spiral fashion—we can visit several stages several times—but there is always a sense of progression. It is almost the same as going around the simple relationship diagram many times, working through issues, refining and maturing the relationship.

The Physical Structure of Relationships

What follows is another simple way of looking at relationships. It is useful to help someone get an understanding of how things are for him or her.

In any relationship there are two entities and a space that represents the relationship. It is in this space that the relationship lives and is experienced.

Each brings into this space what he or she wants to (and what is agreed upon). It is the love that is carried into this space that enables everything. It allows the togetherness, the sharing, the intimacy. It also allows feedback to be given—both pleasant and unpleasant— as the relationship grows. It is in this space that each can be a mirror for the other, and it is here where discussion takes place about what is working and what isn't. Children are brought up in this space.

The following is a diagrammatic representation of this idea.

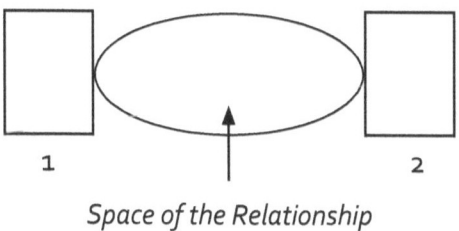

Space of the Relationship

Ideally, individual 1 is happy, healthy, fulfilled and complete. Individual 2 is the same, both having healthy, clear personal boundaries. Whatever else that needs to be in the relationship can be brought in here.

It is essential to know that we are here to live our life's purpose, express ourselves as a reflection of that purpose, and have others around us who help us become more of who we are and less of who we are not.

Knowing this leads to the creation and maintenance of healthy personal boundaries, and that itself defines the kinds of relationships you will have.

Variations:

There are a large number of variables on this theme. We can only explore a few of them here, to illustrate the principle. They are designed to help you get a better understanding of what might happen between two people, and to see how problems might arise.

1. What would happen if this was the arrangement:

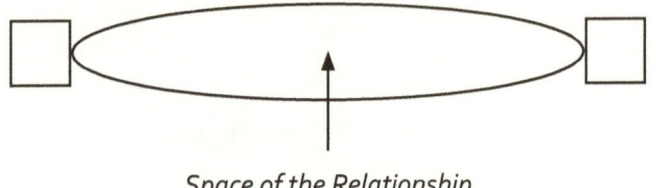

Space of the Relationship

This could happen, for example, if there was any distance between the couple—physically, emotionally or spiritually. Some people keep themselves at a distance—they may not have learned closeness as a child, and they take this pattern into their later lives.

These people don't understand that it is impossible to get close to them. They may be afraid of being vulnerable or hurt, so they opt to keep an emotional distance.

Conversely, there may be valid geographical reasons that keep a couple far apart. Or each partner could come from a very different cultural background, with different expectations of roles, behaviours and so on. This kind of arrangement can work if both parties are comfortable with it. They won't have the closeness that others may want initially; this closeness may come with time. But there are risks. It would be more difficult to keep the space of this relationship style alive, and there is a risk of drifting apart with time.

2. What about this arrangement:

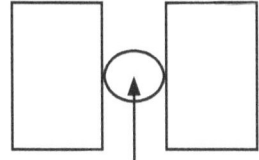

Space of the Relationship

This can typify a relationship in its early exclusive stage. It usually expands into a more dynamic, open type of arrangement.

However, if it stays like that, is there any room there for the relationship to include much? Is this a closeness that inhibits growth? Is it based on fear? The couple can be very joined, but the relationship can be very rigid. The relationship may not be able to handle the fluidity that is demanded from life. It may not allow either party to grow as a human being. This exclusivity may allow little room for others, including children.

3. A *very* close couple may have this kind of arrangement:

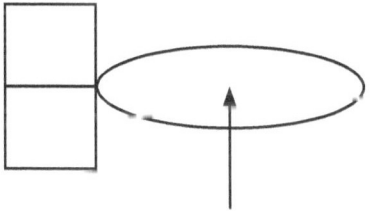

Space of the Relationship

One has to ask what is allowable here? What are its strengths or weaknesses? Perhaps there is agreement on everything; nothing needs to change. Can any growth take place here? This may be something seen in couples who have been together for a very long time, or there is only a single focus or reason for the relationship, and nothing else appears to matter.

4.   Then there is this type of arrangement:

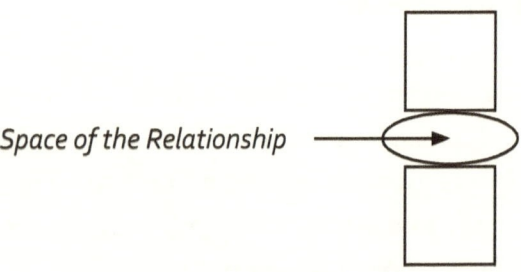

Space of the Relationship

One partner is carrying the other (emotionally or physically). One is completely dependent on another, and the other has somehow accepted that arrangement. This arrangement is very hard to sustain—something is bound to give.

5.   Here's another variation:

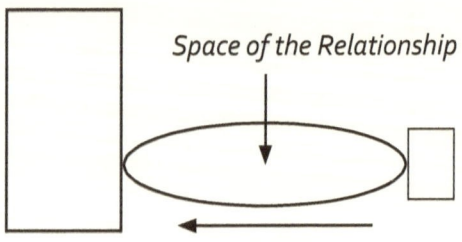

Space of the Relationship

One partner has become subservient, and gives him—or herself totally to the other. One is artificially inflated, the other energetically diminished. There is a flow of energy mainly in one direction. The small rectangle here is at risk of slowly getting smaller, until the position can't be sustained, with inevitable consequences.

6.   Consider the following variation:

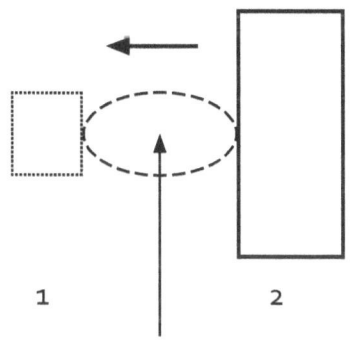

Space of the Relationship

What is unhealthy in this arrangement is that an individual crosses the space, to enter the world of the other. For example, anger in 2 is a high-energy state that tries to overcome resistance to cross over. Lack of respect for the other can lead to a similar result. Physically attacking the other is an extreme example of this.

Helplessness, emptiness, or a lack of self-respect or self-esteem in 1 can also lead to the same result. This is where boundaries are blurred or non-existent, and no one knows the rules. Confusion and unhappiness reigns.

7. This variation is popular at the time of writing:

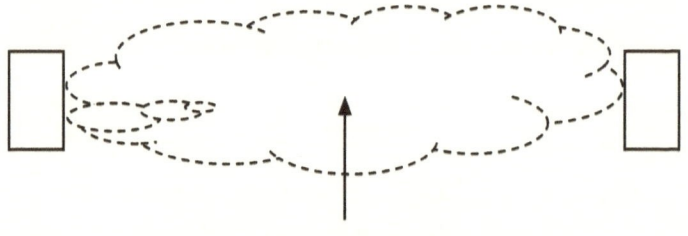

(Cyber)space of the Relationship

The Internet (or cyberspace) relationship!

Arranged relationships could also fit in here. You don't really know what's on the other side initially. Although this can be the beginning of a very successful relationship, it depends on the training, integrity, and honesty of both people—and their determination to make it work. Knowing who you are and what you want is still information you can have with you at all times, especially under these conditions.

In the formation of this type of relationship, there is the clear possibility of the construction of a fantasy that cannot translate into a real-life working relationship.

Sometimes, we want to love so much, that we will give up the reality of potential hurt for these fantasies. Remember that around seventy percent of all communication is the projected energy that goes into the relationship space. About twenty percent of communication is body language and eye contact (the visual clues). Only around ten percent consists of words, either verbal or written. If we rely on ten-to-twenty percent of information only, the chances of getting it right are much lower.

This series of diagrams is not meant to be exhaustive. Rather, it serves as a way of getting you to think about your relationship or relationship style—or even provoke more questions.

How would you draw your prime relationship? Does it help you to understand how it is built and what the rules are that govern it? What's allowed, what isn't.

It could also be useful to make a combination diagram, with different-sized blocks or shapes for the various aspects of a relationship

(iii) Love is present and acknowledged

(iv) Each person allows the possibility that they are wrong, and the other is right

(v) Both partners want to stay in the relationship by choice (and not from outside pressures)

(vi) Both people take responsibility for their roles and actions

(vii) Each person is willing to be real and truthful about everything . . .

then this would provide a great starting place to resolve any issues or problems.

If one party feels differently than the other and wants to persist in some kind of unacceptable behaviour, is the rope irretrievably broken. Can a knot still be tied, even at a great distance in place or time?

We don't know these things. We can only do our best, and take a position that, in our eyes, is true to our truth and not allow any feelings as described previously to block the recognition of this truth.

A broken relationship that is healed has the potential to be even more powerful than it was previously. It

Each type has the ability to express itself in a spectrum—from healthy to unhealthy. The theory states that, "We are born with our particular type; coming in with a certain temperament makes us more likely to respond to our environment in a certain way."

What would be the purpose in identifying what personality type you are? What that does is give you an insight into how you operate in the world. Firstly, the Enneagram shows your strengths, where you are the most effective, and where you are the happiest.

Secondly, it reveals mechanisms you may have adopted at some point in your life to avoid facing hurt or pain. It brings into awareness those tendencies you have that drive you in an unhealthy direction, that are not in your best interests. This is the internal alternative chaos that a younger you may have chosen, perhaps many years earlier.

Knowing your personality type can help you concentrate on your strengths, and avoid behaviours that don't work or cause you to be stressed.

For example, a body type *eight* is depicted in the following way:

For example:

(a) Finances
(b) Work
(c) Parenting
(d) Time together—private or socialising
(e) Individual outside interests
(f) Shared interests
(g) Sex and intimacy
(h) Communication
(i) Home management
(j) Privacy

Look at the discrepancies—one partner may see things one way, the other partner a different way. Are you fulfilled or not in these areas? Have compromises been made, and if so, are they acceptable? Do some areas need particular attention? Perhaps some areas have been avoided out of fear, as described previously.

You could ask yourself questions about the arrangement of your relationships:

Do you tend to cross over into another's territory, or do you stay in your own? Do you want to "fix" things for others, or are you there to help and guide when asked?

Are you the one who always does everything, because no one else can do it as well as you can?

Are you an expert at helplessness who expects the other to do everything? Do you limit someone else's potential by being jealous or possessive? Are you intolerant of others? Dismissive?

Do you help your partner to bring their gifts into the world? Do you sabotage or undermine his or her efforts?

There are many questions that could be asked. They are merely there to get you to look at the relationship in question. They will facilitate finding the key elements in the relationship that need identification, for further action.

Relationship Breakdown

Relationships can break down, of course, at any stage. If this happens during any of the first three initial setup phases, it is usually easier and less stressful. If it breaks down later, it is a different situation.

It is here that conflicts need to be resolved constructively, and responsibility must be taken for one's part in the conflict. If resolution is achieved, then the potential is there for the relationship to move on to function as a healthy, mature ongoing relationship. It then has an inbuilt ability to accept and move with change.

How do the partners in the relationship approach the issues that need attention? What options do they have? It is not really possible for them to go back to being friends, for example—at least not as friends based on the original agreements. Parts of the original contract need to be rewritten.

It is likely that the seeds of what caused the relationship to break down were present from the beginning— they just weren't appreciated or known at the time.

Conversely, they may have been known but considered unimportant. They could have been ignored for fear of not wanting to upset the other or being seen to "rock the boat".

Repair of a Relationship

To recapitulate: what happens if a relationship breaks down? From what was explained previously, once intimacy has been established but broken down, it will be very difficult to go backwards (to being friends), to help rebuild a healthy intimacy; the problem that caused the breakdown is most likely still there.

It may be that you just choose to remain friends as things are. However, if the choice is to clarify what needs attention and re-build the intimacy in the relationship, then a useful strategy would be to complete the circle in the diagram shown previously, and go to *formal* again. There, one has the opportunity to ask the basic question, "Who am I?" again, and it becomes possible to re-negotiate what is allowed in the space of the relationship.

This may last a short or long time, but it is an effective option to explore what possibilities exist.

Going back to *formal* will give you a focus and a safe place to be. From there any issue can be looked at, discussed, worked through and a new place of acceptance can be found. With some issues, it may only take a second to know what is possible or not. With others, committed work by both partners is needed to find a new place of understanding and agreement.

In a healthy relationship, this circle can be negotiated several times. Things that don't work can be discussed and new solutions can be found. Deeper levels of friendship and intimacy can be created in this way.

Sometimes, during this process, what was thought to be a problem may in fact not be. Sometimes expectations are removed, leaving an unimaginable freedom in the relationship. Or, what was acceptable before is now found to be unacceptable. Interests change, values change. It is up to each of us to become clear on these things—and to have the courage to stick to and state our truths in the negotiation that follows.

What's Required:

What then is asked of us? What is required, for us to be able to do the re-building?

I believe this is where we are asked to go inside and look at our 'hot buttons'. Our beliefs, our values, the promises or vows we made to ourselves in earlier times, any expectations we carry (personal, familial, cultural), our relationship style—all these need to be examined.

We need to look at those things that we allowed, even though they were not in our best interests. We need to have the courage and the willingness to do this work, to find out what is not working for us, what is not healthy. We also need the strength to correct the situation to the best of our ability.

This is where the pain is. Feelings we carry—of anger, hurt, blame, hopelessness, helplessness, aloneness, shame and guilt—will surface.

If you think about it, we experience prolonged pain and suffering because we haven't wanted to deal with these feelings before—it is about our resistance. By opening your inner being and welcoming everything enables you to dissolve the resistance, and be free to work on what is required. You can resolve and release the hurt, and come to a new understanding of who you are and what you want.

This process has the ability to clean up boundary issues. We get clear about what we want in our lives, what is acceptable, and we learn how to communicate this to others. We learn how to take risks for ourselves, and to put ourself on the line—for our own self-respect and integrity. We learn where and how to draw the line in a new and healthier way than that which existed before.

The Strength of a Bond

The following is a metaphor for repairing a relationship:

1. Let's say we have a rope. That rope is as strong as it is. No matter what you do to it or with it, it remains essentially as it was from the beginning. The nature of the rope cannot be changed.

2. Now, let's say we cut that rope, and then re-join it by tying a knot. If it is a good knot, then the rope at that point is likely to be stronger than it was before (and therefore stronger than anywhere along its length).

3. Take a relationship with another person. Metaphorically, it contains many ropes—some thick and strong, some perhaps not so, representing different aspects of that relationship. If that relationship generally remains untested, it stays exactly as it always was—like the rope.

    But if something tests the relationship, that causes it to be stressed (or seemingly broken), then with the right knot—the right repair—the relationship can be stronger afterward than it ever was.

4. So what is the right knot? It has to involve a commitment to identify what caused the break, and a willingness to do what it takes to repair it. Both parties have to recognise this, believe it, and work towards it.

5. What could stop this re-bonding from happening? What caused the breakdown may be irretrievable or totally unacceptable (note that I have not said *unforgivable*). All those feelings described before (fear of humiliation, shame, guilt, confusion, and so on) can prevent the repair. Feelings of low self-esteem or low self-confidence can equally prevent re-bonding.

6. It is required that you ask yourself where those feelings come from—including whether they are yours, or whether they are being powerfully projected on to you by another person. You need to know whether these feelings stop you from acknowledging an underlying and more significant truth?

   Ask yourself: "If I can't feel shame (for example), what would I *have* to feel?" This process will lead you down to a core emotion that may initially be difficult to feel or acknowledge. Once accessed, however, you will discover that this is *the* motivating emotion that governs your behaviour in this instance.

Does a feeling of being a failure stop you from even trying? If so, what test have you failed? The fact that we are given tests means that there is always the possibility of success—they are a means to an end.

7. How can negative feelings be resolved and released? Firstly, by allowing them and not blocking or suppressing them; by not stopping them and playing with them. For me, this is emotional intelligence. Secondly, by adopting a different perspective and giving yourself permission to change your attitude and therefore way you see things.

Asking for help often opens doors and facilitates this process.

With respect to a broken relationship then, if one adopts a position where:

(i) True repentance is present
(ii) One is not judgemental or critical in any way

will be a different relationship. It is up to the parties involved to at least investigate this possibility, and if accepted, to believe it, want it and work towards it—with dignity and respect.

Your Relationship with Yourself

We have now discussed who we are, why we are here, why we need relationships in our lives, the structure of relationships, and what choices we have around those relationships (especially if breakdown takes place).

We have also looked at the influences in our lives that can cause us to adopt unhealthy attitudes or behaviours. These in turn may cause a relationship to break down as we have seen. Perhaps there are expectations that can't be met, or perhaps things fall apart because the other person in the relationship is giving us feedback about our behaviour, and we don't like what we hear!

Therefore, knowing yourself as you do, would you want to be in a relationship with someone like yourself? If so, great. If not, why not? What needs to happen, to be able to answer in the affirmative?

Ultimately, it is all about how we see ourselves, how we feel about ourselves, how we feel about how we want to be, and how we want to be received by others.

Judgements and fears contract our energy. When this energy is lowered far enough, we break down and lose our sense of who we are, our sense of self. We need to return to who we are—to expand, to flow, to live fully on the path that we chose and is intended for us.

To start a relationship repair, it is therefore worth asking yourself these three questions again:

1. Who am I?
2. Where am I going?
3. Who do I choose to come with me?

In other words, to repair a relationship with someone else, we first may have to repair the relationship we have with ourselves.

The burden we carry is often the burden of ourselves.
—Eckhart Tolle

I believe that ultimately, the only person you have any jurisdiction over is yourself. You can only work with yourself—you can't ask someone else to change if you aren't willing to do the same.

The reward is that, when you accept this responsibility— when you do work on yourself—you open up into the realm of possibilities. When you 'fix yourself' you will become aware of magic happening all around.

It is as if many of the issues that were present before, resolve of their own accord—without you having to do a thing. This really does work from my experience, and I have seen it working with others countless times.

You may find that by doing this, you discover that the new healthy you finds the current relationship with another unacceptable. That's okay.

Or, you may find that some things need to change. Or, you may discover that what you thought was a problem really isn't one at all. Perhaps you become more tolerant and accepting of your partner. The possibilities are endless; the work required remains the same.

Yes, sometimes you will see loved ones doing silly things, or engaging in behaviours that are unhealthy—behaviours that need to change. You do need to point this out to them, and act appropriately if necessary.

It is still necessary however to look inwards and look at your attitudes and behaviour and correct anything unhealthy you find there. Again, you can't ask anyone to do anything that you are not prepared to do yourself.

I strongly believe that the first step towards sorting anything out is to strip away the masks, the games you play, and the ego—the things you erected to protect yourself from the outside world.

The next step—and another essential ability to have—is to be able to ask for help. It is really hard to look inwards by yourself, to find those memories or those feelings that you have perhaps spent an entire lifetime keeping hidden. Having someone with you allows you to work safely, without having to be your own critic or judge. There is something very powerful in the act of surrender, the act of saying, "I need help." This act of surrender is a prayer to which the universe will always respond.

Some of the things that you can learn along the way are:

1. You never have to sell out to anyone; you can take care of yourself. You don't need the approval of another (or their permission) to feel what you feel, or do what you want to do.

2. There is the experience of gaining (or re-gaining) your self-esteem, your personal power. We all need the experience of being where we don't belong, in

order to understand the importance of being where we *do* belong.

3. You will learn that you can always get out of where you are and go where you truly want to. To do this, you need to bring your energy into the present and not squander it on ruminations of the past or imaginings of the future.

4. At some point on this journey, you will also learn who you are. You will learn that it is enough just to *be* and that there is nothing you have to *do*. This is a state of grace, of enlightenment, and this is where everything starts to fall into place and make sense. This place can be used to re-frame every belief, every experience and every value you hold.

Chaos

Having started to do this work, it is inevitable that you will meet resistance. This comes in various forms, but a lot manifests through the creation of internal "chaos".

Chaos is a form of communication, with others or ourselves. It is really an avoidance technique.

We engage in avoidance when an uncomfortable truth comes too close to us. We deflect it, turn it back towards another, or create an alternative chaos. Chaos can be recognised as anxiety, panic attacks, depression, sleep disorders, obsessions and addictions—for example, food, sex, exercise, work, parties, drugs or fixed routines.

Chaos can also be the filter through which we assess others, leading to the possibility of always attracting others who match that chaos. Those are the people we don't want to meet, which leads to the question, "Why do I always seem to attract the same (wrong) type of person?"

Then there are places of alternative chaos. Those places include areas where you choose not to struggle and go with the will of others (where there is the least amount of trauma).

Or for example, this is where a child will consciously decide to change the way he or she behaves—even if it goes against his or her nature—to get what love and approval they can at the time.

Or, you can choose to try to escape chaos, to escape pain. You can go into fear, denial or shutdown—or even into paralysis—which, by the way, is the most frightening option. Being no one or doing nothing is far worse than trying something and failing or being humiliated. It's tempting to blame someone else for your chaos. However, blaming others is really another avoidance technique.

All these places do not let you be true to yourself. They are often chosen at a very early age, depending on circumstances, parental and peer influences, gender and so on.

Becoming accountable for everything is the essence of true transformation. There we can choose to face up to what is going on inside ourselves, to understand that change needs to happen, and to confront whatever is not working for us.

As I have said before, this requires courage, willingness, trust, and a fierce commitment to do whatever it takes, no matter what. Sometimes of course, life decides for us. Change is imposed on us, whether we want it or not.

It is the struggle to overcome this chaos, this resistance, which embeds the necessary changes in your being, and makes these healthy changes permanent. It is like learning a new skill. At first, it takes concentration and practice, and things are awkward. Then it becomes automatic, and the subconscious takes over, freeing up the body, mind, and emotions.

Looking after the Basics

So, what do you need to understand, where do you need to go, and what do you need to do?

Before undergoing the introspective work required, it is very useful to have the basics looked after. Firstly, let's consider the body.

Are you eating a diet that is healthy for you? Are you aware of how what you eat affects you? *We are what we eat.* It is always useful to check in with your body. It will generally tell you what it needs—whatever that may be.

Getting the physical side of your being into shape can facilitate all sorts of things. It improves your general sense of well-being: you have more energy and you can think more clearly. Improving your physical health has the ability to open up channels to facilitate other energy work that needs to be done. Even though your work may require a lot of physical input, there is still a place for a walk every day to clear your head. Such walks provide needed time, for reflection or meditation. Respect for your body includes appreciating it and using it healthily. Your body is the greatest gift you have been given in this lifetime.

It is also very useful to monitor your language. Remember, speech has the power of creation. What you say reflects your reality, or creates a new one. Be *very* careful, and positive, with your speech. Look out for pressure words (*should, could, must, have to*), words that leave you nowhere (I *hope* that . . . , *maybe* this . . .), and words that make you small, like *sorry* or *can't*.

If speech follows your thoughts, the same reasoning applies here as well. Unspoken thoughts still represent your beliefs—what you believe about yourself, and who you think you are.

Understanding Self

There are many systems or ways of looking at the fundamental psychological makeup of human beings.

The following way is one that appeals to me because it has that essence of truth about it—that *something* that we intuitively recognise as being correct. In practice, it seems to work well.

Don Riso and Russ Hudson of the Enneagram Institute (*references 7, 8*) talk about understanding your personality type as a key to understanding how and why you make your life decisions. They call this the filter through which everything that happens to you, happens.

They then go on to explain that the path to enlightenment is through self-knowledge. And this can be found through what they call the Enneagram (from the Greek: *ennea*, meaning nine; *grammos* meaning diagram), a nine-pointed figure.

The Enneagram is a highly sophisticated system that describes personality types, separated into three groups: *feeling* types, *mind* types and *body* types, each of which has three points (for a total of nine basic personality types). There are detailed descriptions of each type at the Enneagram Institute site. They are depicted in this way:

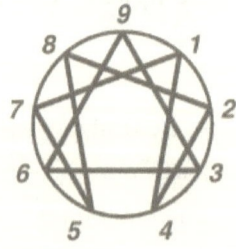

Types 2, 3 and 4 are the *emotional* types, 5,6 and 7 are the *mind* types, and 8,9 and 1 are the *body* types. The lines are called "lines of integration" (working to your strengths) and "lines of disintegration" (working to your weaknesses).

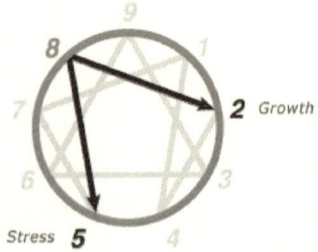

Eights tend to be powerful, dominating types — self-confident, decisive, wilful and confrontational. This type of person may have a fundamental behaviour of turning to anger to escape a painful or threatening situation.

However, if a person with this personality type can learn to use love and compassion, he or she can become a very powerful force for good. *Eights* tend to get stressed and less effective if they go into their minds. The Enneagram provides this kind of information (and much more) for each type.

By identifying your unhealthy behaviours, you now have the knowledge to make choices and correct them. It is then a natural step to find out what it was in your earlier life that caused this all to happen.

And that brings you full circle to uncovering and resolving old hurts, promises or vows you made, or beliefs you adopted that have caused you to behave in the way that you do.

To recap: awareness that there is something in your life that needs attention, that is unhealthy for you, can come in various ways. Awareness can come through your own observation (for example studying the Enneagram), by being told by another directly, by a physical, emotional, or psychological illness, in therapy, or simply by a failed relationship (where something wasn't right, but you didn't know what).

The question now is, what can be done about it? The goal, as I have said, is to find the quintessential self and live as an expression of that. This is real power and real freedom.

This is the point at which the relationship with yourself can really begin to heal, and grow. And when you ask for help, usually the most appropriate way will present itself. A teacher will present him—or herself, a traditional or alternative therapy will become available. Something will come; you can trust and depend on this.

By knowing yourself, you create healthy boundaries for yourself. Once you have established those, then you are free to be yourself within them.

And lastly, our minds work with three things—fear, doubt and judgement—to protect us from hurt. There are times, however, when we need to experience hurt so that we can resolve and release it, so we can be free of it. At these times, our minds may get in the way.

To help remember what *mind* is really all about, remember what each function really is:

FEAR: Fantasy **E**xpectations **A**ppearing **R**eal

DOUBT: Driving **O**urselves **U**nconscious **B**y **T**hinking.

JUDGEMENT : **J**ust **U**n**D**oing **G**od's **E**ternal **M**anagement plan, **E**ntails **N**eedless **T**rouble

Remember too, that using *mind* keeps you in a state of separateness, of *me* and *them*. It can foster a sense of something lacking in your life. Not being in a state of fear, doubt or judgement actually leaves you free to feel connected to everything, and free to explore all possibilities—including the unconditional love that is always there for you.

The bottom line is that, after all this work, this information is there to help you awaken to the possibilities of your own potential, and get you to ask yourself the following: "Am I living my life to the fullest? Am I relaxed and enjoying each moment?

What games am I playing, what do they cost me, and do I want to continue playing them? What's in the way of me being me? Does fear, doubt or judgement run my life?"

And, to keep you focused and grounded, remember to keep asking yourself, "What does this moment require of me?"

Accept what cannot be changed; you have no responsibility to change or reform anyone else. You don't have to accept abuse. But, you do have this responsibility for yourself—to live your ideals in harmony with your soul, your spirit, the Divine.
—Dr C. Norman Shealy

Knowing Who You Are

Right throughout this book, I have used the following phrases: "know yourself" and "know who you are". You can find that out with introspective therapies. You can complete the questionnaire associated with the Enneagram. Or, you can just be aware of everyday experiences that give you clues—if not direct information. Whatever approaches you use, by the time you have *really* looked at all the different aspects of yourself, you *will* know who you are.

You know you are being who you are when something feels *right*. It is also when your responses come from your truth within. They are not reactions—they are responses that make you feel authentic and in integrity with yourself. It feels good when you express yourself in this way. And there is a sense of non-attachment as well—as if you are saying, "This is who I am, and that is what is important to me. No more, no less".

Awareness of who you are can come from being involved in any activity where you surrender yourself and experience a sense of being lost in the moment, and something else takes over—your soul! Your energy seems to be not only inside yourself, but also outside, all around. Doing an act of kindness is a good example.

Knowing yourself is to find yourself in stillness.
Without thought, without noise—a state of simple
alert attention.
—Eckhart Tolle

In other words, when you do something that is effortless—something that makes you feel good—that is when you are probably in touch with your true self. When you feel you are not trying, that whatever you do or say seems to come from a deeper place, when something you do or say feels perfect—that is when you are in touch with your essence. It is beyond beliefs or thoughts; it is just *there*. This is where you find yourself.

The privilege of a lifetime is being who you are.
—Joseph Campbell

Help and Guidance

To deal with all that life has given us, we can trust that there will always be help to count on—and that it is always present. There are guides and teachers that accompany us on this life's journey, that help us every step of the way. Some will stay with us throughout the whole journey; others will be there for some of the way, as needed. This help can come very obviously (through comments people make or other life events), or perhaps more subtly, such as through intuition. The help can also come through a sudden understanding, or epiphany. It can be someone or something that just makes us feel joyful or complete. Sometimes, we can literally ask a question before going to sleep, and wake up with the answer.

Generally, we just have to learn how to listen to the signals that come our way. It is like having a radio—the radio waves are always out there. We have to use our "tuner" and dial in to the correct frequency to hear what we need to.

To help receive these signals, we need to be constantly aware and open. We can also create situations that are conducive to receiving this information and finding out what we need to hear.

All of the following can be effective: finding a quiet space with time for yourself, dropping into meditative reflection, praying, or just going for a walk. In all cases, by staying open, you can ask the questions you want to ask and be receptive for the answers. I have included a simple meditation at the end of the book as an example, to help reach that place of stillness and receptivity.

Next, the choice we have is whether to act on the guidance we get, or not to. What would make you *not* listen to your guidance? Fear of change? Fear of the unknown? Saying no to this opportunity inevitably has consequences in the future.

Regret: the feeling you get, when you have asked for and received, Divine guidance, and then said no.
—Anonymous

Accepting this guidance on the other hand—and acting on it—will bring about a speed of change in your life that can take your breath away. It is time to act on something, when it won't leave you alone.

And remember: destiny will take over if you do not act on your guidance or intuition. You are given time, but if you don't act, it will. And it will destroy your reality, because it's time for you to move on.

Guidance in the guise of enforced change can come into your life, by losing your job for example, or a relationship or business fails, or by losing money or property unexpectedly. You may have to ask yourself why you were so attached to what it was that has been lost—and how important it *really* was.

Once you have accepted this as guidance—as soon as you acknowledge or admit to it—then you are responsible for it! And as soon as you are responsible, you have to act. That is a universal truth.

Procrastination or laziness are habits we have to delay admitting the truth, being responsible, and taking action. Don't be vague with yourself. Be specific, be honest, be accurate. Be focussed. The more focussed and the more detached and objective you become, the more effective you are. Choose this path.

Questions that will help you decide what to do, are: "What does this moment require? Who do I really have to be? What do I really have to do right now?" These questions bypass fear or any other resistance, and leave you free to know what to do next.

In addition, remember that the help you are being given is exactly right for where you are in your life. If you are just starting on the path that is the right one for you, the universe will respond in kind. If you are further along, the universe will give you that much more help. If you are well down the right path, life will appropriately pour whatever resources it has to help keep you moving that way.

Conversely, if you are just off the right path, the universe will organise things so that you stay there, and so on. Therefore, if you are way off the right path, you will find that everything that happens to you seems to stop you getting back to where you really belong. This is the way life works.

Turning around from this place is difficult, but not impossible. It is choice or free will that is always there to use, to keep you going. Choice also allows you to ask for help.

I see this all the time. People who are, for whatever reason, in the deepest holes of life, somehow find that part of themselves—call it human dignity, or the human spirit—that helps them decide that there *is* a point to life. They realise that there *is* still something special to be experienced, and there are still people to love. They show enormous courage by climbing out of the deepest darkness and despair that they are in. They choose to face whatever they have to, to rebuild their lives, and find meaning and purpose again. They are heroes.

Forgiveness

One of the most powerful and transformational tools we have is the act of forgiveness. This is often misunderstood. Once understood, this act can be used in its most effective way—and it is one of the great gifts you can give yourself.

Forgiveness is a term that everyone knows. We know that we should practise it, but what does it actually mean? What does it involve?

When we are hurt by another, it is a common perception that we should be able to 'turn the other cheek' and walk away. We are expected to 'forget' that we have been harmed, to not retaliate against the perpetrator of that harm and move on

But I don't believe this is the true meaning of the word. It is not saying, "What you did to me was okay". It is more complicated than that, and it requires an understanding of what is involved and the desired outcome.

Beginning from first principles: what happens when we are hurt by another person and blame them or feel vengeful towards them? We invest energy into that state—part of our spirit then resides with that person and we have literally given our power over to them.

We can become consumed in maintaining that state. These feelings we carry will then need constant attention and this costs us energy. As mentioned before, it is like trying to keep a balloon under water. As long as we supply energy and concentrate on it, we keep it there. As soon as we get distracted, up it comes—and it takes effort to get it back down. This drain of energy keeps us tired and sick inside. Not to be able to forgive is an act of revenge, and revenge is really an avoidance technique that prevents you from feeling what is truly there. Maintaining the revengeful state robs you of energy and power. It also stops you from finding and experiencing love.

Reaction to stored vengeance, shame, regret, bitterness, fear or anger associated with unfinished business, is the cause of much illness.

We need to take responsibility for that which is ours, but we do not have to carry anything that belongs to someone else. For example, the anger and fear behind bullying belongs to the bully, not us. Being responsible only for what is ours puts us in control of our lives, our feelings, and our thoughts.

Just to illustrate how we do carry people around with us, Caroline Myss, in her book *Entering the Castle* describes it well. I like it because it is so simple and so revealing. She describes a scene wherein you enter your own "castle" (representing the soul). You work your way down the various corridors of this castle until you come to the dungeons. There you find those people whom you have kept imprisoned, for the hurt they caused you in the past. You also remember how long they have been imprisoned there. She then asks you to ask yourself, "How much energy has it cost me to keep them down here, and what would it feel like to simply open the cell door and let them out? How much freer and lighter would I feel?" I have yet to meet anyone who didn't have someone down there.

We really need to know how to complete our interactions with others appropriately without any (so-called) residual negative feelings. We are then free to be who we are, and move on.

> *You can't perfect your world, whilst you harbour*
> *thoughts of harm against others.*
> *—Wayne Dyer*

Secondly, it is clear to me that each and every one of us is born with a purpose. We all have a role to fulfil and a gift to bring into the world—to help us grow as individuals, and make the world a better place. To bring this gift into the world, we often have to go through struggle, even pain. In fact, the hurt itself can be a divine gift wrapped in this particular way.

It seems that struggling through the hurt brings an essential part of ourselves into clear focus that we then have to deal with. This can be our courage or our ability to feel compassion, for example. We learn to appreciate this part, how to use it, and learn that it is fundamental to who we really are, and that in turn builds self-confidence and leads to enhanced sense of self-worth.

Given all that, our lives are set up perfectly for each and every one of us. We are faced with the exact challenges we need at all times, to manifest our gifts and promote continual growth in self-knowledge and wisdom. All the hardships, all the traumas are part of this grand design.

If this is true, then all the people we meet who place difficulties in our paths—those who cause us pain, either deliberately or inadvertently—must be part of this scenario. Even those who abuse us or cause us great sorrow.

We may never know the reason why bad things happen to us, why things appear unfair. And accidents, which are not part of any plan, can occur (but that doesn't mean we don't have to do the work—we still do). It doesn't matter. We are always obliged to accept that everything that happens to us happens for a reason, even though we may not be able to see that at the time—or perhaps ever. Whatever the case, there is learning and understanding in *every* event in our lives. We always have to deal with whatever happens in a way that is in line with our truth and sense of justice and self-respect.

Colin Tipping in his book *Radical Forgiveness*, states, *"Whereas traditional forgiveness remains committed to the idea of there being a victim and a perpetrator, radical forgiveness recognises that things happen not TO us, but FOR us".*

So, with every event in your life (be it pleasant or unpleasant) learn to ask yourself, "How come this is happening? What's the reason for it? What am I being asked to learn?" These questions instantly change your position with respect to the hurt—you are now a student of your life, and not a victim of it. Forgiving the person or persons involved, automatically enables you to be in your own power. In effect, we bring that part of our spirit that has been lost or abandoned back to ourselves in the present. It is saying, "I forgive you because you are just the messenger", or "I forgive you because you are here to help me".

These are the questions that bring light into the darkness, and using them stops us from collapsing into the hurt we feel, making it a burden we have to carry and giving it power over ourselves. None of us are absolved from doing this work. And the closer we are to success, to conquering the pain, the harder things may appear to be. That's the way it is—the darkest part of the night is just before dawn.

Forgiveness undoes all illusion. It is the pathway to wellness and self-empowerment, and it is a powerful act of spiritual transformation.

Forgiveness is when you yourself let go of the story. It is in the forgiving, that we ourselves are forgiven—we are released and healed. It enables us to move from a low energy state into a higher energy state. The act of forgiveness is always instructive and it *is* liberating.

This I believe is the way to enlightenment, a pathway we can choose in everyday life. It's all between you and yourself (or God, if that is your belief) anyway; it was never between you and them.

Forgiveness is the art of retrieving your spirit and returning it into present time. Forgiveness is the ultimate and most powerful act of personal spiritual alchemy. It completely transforms your cell memory, and helps you to re-write the code that is managing your biology so that the future cell tissue that spins off from that cell no longer has the toxic memory inside. Therefore it no longer has the code for producing illness.
—Caroline Myss

Forgiveness doesn't let the other off the hook; it lets you off the hook. It frees you from the burden of unnecessary and unwanted feelings. It allows you to leave a relationship with someone who hurt you. If you condemn someone, who are you truly condemning?

Forgiveness is the fragrance that the violet sheds on the heel that has crushed it.
—Mark Twain

A metaphor for life that I like is this one: We can know the sentence, we can know the page or paragraph, we can even know the chapter, but we will never know the book. That is hidden from us in this physical existence.

Life is like arriving late for a movie, having to figure out what was going on without bothering everybody with a lot of questions, and then being unexpectedly called away before you find out how it ends.
—Joseph Campbell

We may not understand at the time how and why things have to be the way they are, but that doesn't take anything away from the truth of things—there will always be things that we find hurtful; the game of life never stops.

Looking at the converse for a moment, do we have to run around—perhaps once a year—asking those whom we believe we have hurt, for forgiveness?

I couldn't answer that categorically, but I could perhaps ask instead, how come you really want to ask the other for forgiveness? Where are they, in their lives, in relation to the event? Have they moved on? Are you the one who is stuck? Did it bother them at all? Is it your guilt or shame? Can forgiveness occur without direct conversation?

Self-forgiveness

Which brings us to the subject of self-forgiveness. This may be the hardest act of forgiveness to do. It is easier to forgive someone else than to forgive yourself. We are generally far harder on, more critical of, and more judgemental of ourselves than we are of anyone else.

In forgiving yourself you are making a statement: "I am not the same person today as the one who committed that wrong. I have changed, and such an act no longer defines the person I am now.

I look back at the person who committed that wrong, and I no longer see myself in him or her or identify with that act." (This same reasoning, of course, applies to anyone else as well.)

This should be followed by an acknowledgement of yourself—that you may have been doing the best you could with the resources you had at the time. Understand that there is a younger you whose behaviour you now disapprove of, who wants to be loved by you. They want to be released from the isolation you may have left them in and brought home.

Remember that, had you been in the younger self's shoes, you probably would have done the same!

What are the ingredients necessary for self-forgiveness to take place?

There are three elements:

1) Admission: admit that you did something that was not in alignment with your true nature, which hurt yourself or someone else. Specifically identify what it is that you have done.

2) Confession: own responsibility for what has been done.

3) Repentance: commit to change so that you will never repeat that behaviour again. Recognise that you have changed, that you are not the person you used to be, and that you will never go back.

To support the act of forgiveness, do an act of kindness. This will strengthen your whole being, plus that of the receiver (and anyone else who observes that act).

It moves you from a state of illness (I-centred) to a state of wellness (we-centred), or well-being.

And finally, there is an additional way: allow yourself to be the unconditional love that you are, and feel it for yourself and others. That's all.

"Our deepest fear is not that we are inadequate. Our deepest fear is that we are powerful beyond measure. It is our light, not our darkness that most frightens us. We ask ourselves, Who am I to be brilliant gorgeous, talented, fabulous?

Actually, who are you not to be? You are a child of God. Your playing small doesn't serve the world.

There is nothing enlightened about shrinking so that other people won't feel insecure around you. We are all meant to shine, as children do. We are born to manifest the glory of God within us. It is not just in some of us. It's in everyone, and as we let our own light shine, we unconsciously give other people permission to do the same. As we are liberated from our own fear, our presence automatically liberates others".

—Marianne Williamson

Your Relationship with Spirit

What is our spirit? What is this part of us? Why is there even a need to have a relationship with this part of ourselves? What does this mean anyway? By *spirit* or *soul*, I don't mean our anima or life force. I mean that part of us that resides outside the physical, but is an intimate and very real part of who we are.

It is that part of us that gives us the ability to have imagination, get ideas, and provide inspiration. It is where we get our sense of humour and refinement of thought. It is non-ego and non-personality.

This is the part of ourselves that gives us insight and perspective, the part that helps us understand the meaning and purpose of our lives.

This is where a sense of greatness comes in, where we see that we are part of something much bigger than we are. It is here where we can step outside our own limitations and start to understand just how powerful and accomplished we can be.

Our relationship with this part of ourselves is not merely a luxury or optional exercise. It is the difference between a meaningless existence and a meaningful one. It is the difference between becoming who we really are (with all our gifts) or remaining an empty shell. It is the difference between leaving a permanent mark on this world or dissolving into oblivion.

A simple exercise is to imagine yourself sitting high above the world, with a mentor, for example. Looking way down at the place where you live (with all its physical attributes and the people in your life), the conversation up here would not be about the details of your physical existence. Rather, it is much more likely to be about meaning and purpose: "What is the reason those people are in my life? What have they come to teach me? What am I helping them to learn? What is my life's purpose?" This is your spirit or highest self at work.

If this is the case, how do we know how to access this part of ourselves in everyday life?

This is a matter for each individual; there are orthodox and unorthodox avenues for this. We must always seek out wisdom, of course, from teachers and mentors, as well as look for answers within ourselves.

But no matter how we choose to access the information that comes our way, we all have spiritual antennae to use—the ability to tune in to our inner voice or guidance. These antennae come with various names, such as *gut feeling* or *intuition*. We need the ability to ask ourselves at any given moment how we feel about an experience, or the information we are being given. Another way of accessing this spiritual guidance is to ask ourselves a specific question, with a 'yes' or 'no' outcome, and see how we respond.

Using mindfulness techniques are also useful. Mindfulness is a mental state of openness, awareness and focus. It is used to reduce stress and raise self-awareness, for example. It also enables us to be able to be aware of what there is in the moment and, in this state of openness, become aware of what our truth is. Any required action will follow automatically and appropriately.

One should establish mindfulness in one's day-to-day life maintaining as much as possible a calm awareness of one's bodily functions, sensations (feelings), objects of consciousness (thoughts and perceptions), and consciousness itself. The practice of mindfulness supports analysis resulting in the arising of wisdom.
—The Buddha

Another useful exercise is to remind ourselves that we are able to choose at all times. We need to be able to ask ourselves at all times, "What do I choose right now, in this moment, that will help me to be more of who I am? What is intuitively right? What feels good?"

These questions help us to differentiate between needs and wants, and force us to distinguish for ourselves what we must choose—as well as when and why. We have to be able to access that wisdom to help us choose what is the best for ourselves at any given moment. I am not referring to the ability to choose based on cognitive information. Rather I am referring to our ability to tune in to inspiration or intuition.

We have to understand that the battle in life is between the desires of the body and the aspirations of the spirit. There are times when you know objectively that something is good for you, but your physical desires get in the way and distort your outlook.

The ultimate desire of the body is to take it easy, to escape and exist in perpetual comfort rather than make the effort to confront life head-on. The ultimate desire of the spirit is to live fully and vibrantly with every fibre of your being, to do what's meaningful, what's right, what's productive.

Identify with your spirit. Your spirit is the real you!

If you can identify with the desires of the spirit, it will satisfy the needs of the real you. Your task is to train the body and coax it to reflect the reality of the spirit.

Use the same strategy that the body uses on you! The body says, "Just one bite of cake." You respond, "Sure! In just ten minutes", and then you push it off another ten minutes. Don't say, "I am hungry", say, "My body is hungry." Identify with your spirit and make your body a reflection of it. If you do that, it is the path to real inner peace.

Given all of the above—given that we have free will, the ability to choose and grow as humans—what is the purpose? Where does this all take us?

The ultimate use of our free will is to become a partner in the ability of all of us to perfect the world.

And then, the ultimate goal of having free will is to give it away, to become a servant to that greater power that resides in all of us . . . to manifest spirituality in this physical world.

The ultimate goal is to achieve perfection in all human attributes, to be able to re-join Spirit and become part

of the Infinite. To move from being a 'Child of God' to an 'Adult of God.'
—*Steve Bhaerman*

That is when we become the most effective, the most powerful. Remember, if we consider ourselves physical beings, we have limited resources that can become depleted.

If we allow ourselves to become part of and have access to the infinite energy, there are no limits. We have access to unlimited energy, unlimited potential. That's exciting.

One final thought: consider what it would mean if this relationship with your spirit were allowed to permeate all other relationships. What extra dimension would that bring, if any? What if we all lived in an awareness that all our thoughts and actions were subject to this scrutiny?

Would that change any aspect of any relationship we have, with ourselves, with our spouse, with our children, with our family or friends or neighbours, or society at large? Or the planet or entire universe?

Questions and Reminders

Asking yourself these questions can keep you grounded and centred, focussed on who you are and how to keep yourself there, and therefore more effective in life:

> "What energy do I need today?"
> "What's stopping me from knowing what I need to know?"
> "What's distracting me?"
> "What tasks do I need to complete, and with whom?"

"What do I feel I need to do, right now? What does this moment require of me?"

And then these:

> "What warmth and support do I have around me?"
> "What can I do today that would bring meaning and purpose into my life?"
> "Is there a sense of contribution to the well-being of others, in what I do?"

And especially: "What would really turn me on and be exciting to do, no matter what?"

I would also recommend keeping the following as part of your everyday life:

i. Be filled with appreciation and gratitude for everything that is in your life.

ii. Do an act of kindness every day.

iii. If you want something really badly in your life, help someone else to get the same thing.

There are no quick-fix solutions; this book was not designed to provide that. It was designed to provide a framework of ideas and tools, so that by applying the techniques described, and (especially) doing your best to work at answering as many of the questions asked as you can, you can find your own truth, and use that as a way to reveal who you really are, and find and enjoy the most meaningful relationships you can.

Summary

Summarising the main points so far:

(a) I believe it is useful to constantly ask yourself the following questions on a regular basis. Thinking about the answers can keep relationships dynamic and healthy:

> "Who am I?"
> "Where am I going?"
> "Who do I want to come with me?"

And remember to keep the questions in this order.

(b) Always start with the relationship you have with yourself. Before you try to analyse why a relationship with someone else is not working for you, it is important to find out what it is that makes you think the way you think, feel the way you feel, and do the things you do. These answers will let you know why you react in the way you do.

(c) Remember that *nothing* is written in stone. Everything you believe, think, feel, or do can be changed. You are not your feelings, you are not your beliefs, and you are not your thoughts. These are things that come and go. You are who you are—think about it. Accepting this is the first step towards enlightenment.

(d) You will feel afraid when you leave the known and step into the unknown. This is normal. If you can accept the fear unconditionally, and allow yourself to feel it, it will pass. It will leave you free to explore the possibilities that arise. The present is really the unknown; as soon as something becomes known, it is the past.

(e) Once you have become completely at ease with who you are—knowing precisely what you want in your life and for what reasons—then you are free to build any relationship you want. It is very likely you will attract someone in exactly the same position.

(f) There are times when you will fail. That's life. You are required to pick yourself up, try again, and keep going. Each time we fail, we can fail better. These tests are there to help us grow. If they weren't there, life would be static and pointless. And they are called tests, because they *can* be passed.

Remember: "Only the worthy are tested."

(g) None of this is abstract or hard. It is all do-able. It just requires focus, determination, and perseverance on your part. With these qualities you will inevitably succeed.

(h) You can work with yourself, or another. Remember: the help you want is *always* at hand. You merely have to ask, and the act of asking for help will open up doors you could never have dreamt of.

Set simple goals for yourself—perhaps just being aware of your feelings at all times (or being aware of your reactions).

Ask yourself, "What is driving my thoughts or actions?" "What am I *really* feeling, and where does that come from?" You will learn to be your own observer. Insights will come, and there you are—you are on your way.

If I had to offer more practical advice, it would be the following:

1. Communicate your love for others. We are not judged by our thoughts or feelings; we are judged by our actions. Pay people compliments; do special things for them.

2. The most effective way to be loved is to *be* the unconditional love that you are. When you give pleasure of any variety—whether it be physical, material, emotional, or spiritual, —with no strings attached, they will love you. Giving others pleasure provides the giver with a tremendous source of pleasure. And those observing these acts will feel just as good!

   Giving pleasure gives life purpose and meaning, because we see the positive impact we can make. Do the unexpected; perform acts of kindness. Demonstrating your love not only changes the receiver, it changes the giver.

   Showing compassion, not embarrassing anyone, not gossiping, showing respect—it all works.

3. As far as intimacy goes, a prerequisite to being loved is the inner decision to allow yourself to be loved. This, in turn, means that you have to open yourself to being hurt—and you have to allow the possibility of getting to know yourself better.

4. As for wisdom, this is the greatest gift you can give to someone. The right insight given can change someone's life forever. Whenever you learn a piece of wisdom, think how you can apply

it to give someone else pleasure. Learn to give it appropriately. Focus on the person to whom you are speaking and make it relevant to that person.

If you can see all this at all times, I believe it is a big step towards understanding that you are always a student of life and never a victim of it. We are here in this life to learn, grow, experience joy, have fun, and make the world a better place.

Do not follow where the path may lead.
Go instead where there is no path and leave a trail.
—Ralph Waldo Emerson

Meditation

Bring down a beam of beautiful golden light, see it as a waterfall tumbling over you. Feel its protection. Feel this light filling your body, from your toes, up your legs, up your body, down your arms, and up to your head.

Feel this golden yellow, feel the power, feel the guidance it brings. Feel the intuitive wisdom it is bringing to you.

Say in your own words: "I bless and release all memories and fears of the past. I step into the canoe that is beside the river". See the canoe that has pulled into the shore. See in the canoe, comfortable cushions of all colours. Step into the canoe, and recline, feeling safe and peaceful.

Feel the boat move from the shore into the river, and know there are no oars. Let the river take you where it will, through the rapids, into the gently flowing waters, and then into a still lake. Know that you will return in God's time, not before. Just allow yourself to drift, on the current, drawing the warm gold of the sun, as it shines down on you.

Feel the wisdom of God's hand touch you, and then feel the boat turn with the tide and go back whence it came— leaving the lake, up through the river, back through the rapids, where it pulls into the shore all by itself.

And as you alight from the canoe, you sit on the green grass, you sit cross-legged, and you thank God for the healing and wisdom that has been imparted to you and the knowledge that control is actually beyond control.

That you've given up, and you allow God to guide you. That you awake each day, and say: "I wonder what's in store today?" Blessing it and thanking it before it has even come, without knowing what it is.

Allow the wonderment of a child to carry you through the day, and at the end, count every blessing and be ever grateful for what you have been given, because it will have been far more than you ever dreamed of.

And then bring your attention to the golden light, and feel it closing around you and sealing in all that golden energy, until the next time you come.

References

1. Bays, Brandon. The Journey. (Thorsons, 1999). http://www.thejourney.com

2. Grille, Robin. "What Your Child Remembers: New discoveries about early memory and how it affects us". Sydney's Child, Volume 14, No 4 (May, 2003). http://www.nospank.net/grille5.htm

3. Harder, Arlene F. "The Developmental Stages of Erik Erikson". http://childdevelopmentinfo.com/child-development/erickson.shtml

4. Moorjani, Anita. Dying To Be Me: My Journey from Cancer, to Near Death, to True Healing. (Hay House, 2012).

5. Levine A, Heller RSF. "Get Attached". *Scientific American Mind*, January / February 2011. http://www.scientificamerican.com/article.cfm?id=get—attached

6. Jacobson S. Forty-nine steps to personal refinement. Meaningful Life Centre, Brooklyn, New York. http://www.meaningfullife.com

7. The Enneagram Institute: http://www.enneagraminstitute.com/

8. Riso, Don Richard and Russ Hudson. The Wisdom of the Enneagram. (Bantam Books, 1999).